UNPLUGGED ACTIVITIES FOR FUTURE CODERS

BUILD YOUR UX AND UI DESIGN SKILLS

Christopher Harris

Illustrations by Joel Gennari

Enslow Publishing
101 W. 23rd Street
Suite 240
New York, NY 10011
USA

enslow.com

Published in 2020 by Enslow Publishing, LLC.
101 W. 23rd Street, Suite 240, New York, NY 10011

Library of Congress Cataloging-in-Publication Data

Names: Harris, Christopher, author. | Gennari, Joel, illustrator.
Title: Build your UX and UI design skills / Christopher Harris ;
illustrations by Joel Gennari.
Description: New York : Enslow Publishing, 2020. | Series: Unplugged
activities for future coders | Includes bibliographical references and
index. | Audience: Grades 5-8.
Identifiers: LCCN 2018055033| ISBN 9781978510715 (library bound) | ISBN
9781978510708 (pbk.)
Subjects: LCSH: User interfaces (Computer systems)
Classification: LCC QA76.9.U83 H366 2019 | DDC 005.4/37—dc23
LC record available at https://lccn.loc.gov/2018055033

Printed in the United States of America

To Our Readers: We have done our best to make sure all website addresses in this book were active and appropriate when we went to press. However, the author and the publisher have no control over and assume no liability for the material available on those websites or on any websites they may link to. Any comments or suggestions can be sent by email to customerservice@enslow.com.

Image Credits: Character illustrations by Joel Gennari, other art by Christine Pekatowski.

CONTENTS

INTRODUCTION

Think about what happens when you turn on your computer. After a few loading screens, you arrive at the desktop. It's here you can find the shortcuts and buttons you use every day. Whether you're opening your favorite browser or loading up the newest game, these shortcuts and buttons are the foundation of your typical computer use. But have you ever thought about what all these tools are actually doing?

A computer's desktop is an example of a user interface (UI). Broadly, this term refers to the way through which you (the user) are able to interact (or interface) with your computer. In particular—unless you use an advanced operating system—your desktop is a graphical user interface (GUI). This just means that the UI you're looking at uses pictures (or graphics) to convey information. A shortcut for a computer game, for example, might have a picture of the hero as its icon—and instead of having to type out a complex command to tell your computer to open the game, you can simply click the shortcut in the GUI.

This ease of use is one reason why nearly every computer, smartphone, and tablet in the world uses a GUI. Designers of successful products—whether hardware or software—are very interested in improving the user experience (UX). UX deals with how a user moves through an app—inputting data and getting back results, working within different sections—and gets their task done. If you have ever struggled to complete a task in a program, it may have felt like the program was bugged or broken. Or, it might have just had a poorly designed overall UX, possibly related to its UI.

For the most positive UX, programmers pay attention to the placement of menus, buttons, and other text elements in their UI. After all, if their software is confusing, people simply won't use it.

In addition to how easy and intuitive it is to use an application, UX and UI designers are also concerned with the general look and overall feel of their software. Think back to your computer's desktop—is everything drab, gray, and dull? More likely, it's colorful, varied, and vibrant. Each of your shortcuts probably has a unique icon that not only looks good, but also conveys to you—the user—exactly what that shortcut is going to do. In a modern GUI, the user is able to immediately and consistently recognize the programs they want to launch based on the information they are presented. At least, that's the goal.

One way to help you start to think more about UX and UI is to analyze the programs and websites you use daily. When you open up your favorite game or go to a website, are you clear on what each button, link, or similar element will do within the program or where it will take you? Are you ever surprised by the result of clicking a button or following a link? Those are sure signs of poor UX or UI design. You may have the experience necessary to correct the mistakes of the UX designer, but think about your parents or grandparents. Would they be able to go back and notice where they went wrong? The job of the UX designer is to make sure that everyone, regardless of their experience with computers, programming, or technology, can quickly and easily understand and use their application.

Designing an app in a way that makes sense sounds easy, but it can definitely be tricky. This is especially true because different styles of software will require different UI layouts and UX goals. A shopping website might need a few easy buttons to add items to a virtual shopping cart, but what about your school's website? By the same token, links to teacher biographies and homework help guides would be out of place on a shopping website. And even further, a website guide for novice computer scientists is going to look a lot different than an advanced video course for seasoned software developers! Every project has its own ins, outs, and design guidelines, so a good UX designer is absolutely critical to the success of an application.

Now that you understand the importance of a good UX and a good UI—and how they're related—this book is going to help refine your skills. Because design work is often not strictly related to any particular programming language, you can learn about good design practices using a pencil and paper—no computer needed.

BECOME A UI DESIGNER

 10–15 minutes

 1 player

YOUR MISSION

Imagine this situation: Your best friend is planning an event and has asked you to design a digital flyer to post online so everyone can learn about the event. But you don't know anything about designing flyers! Lucky for you, you're about to learn how to make a good UI that will draw attention to the event.

Your Gear

- **Drawing supplies**
- **Paper**

LET'S PLAY

Designing user interfaces is an art! If your digital product is supposed to appeal to a wide range of people, there are some guidelines you should follow. There are some things people just love to see. Your digital flyer should include at least some of the following features:

- Colors that complement each other and the type of event
- A font that matches the feeling of the event
- A large title

Though every good UI designer needs to have strong coding skills, many of the best also have incredible artistic vision—and the two are not as different as you might think! A programmer needs to be able to envision their final product, create the code necessary, and construct their program. Similarly, artists start with nothing more than an idea and take the necessary steps to accomplish their expression. The end result for both coders and artists is something everyone can enjoy. As you work to design UIs and UXs, make sure you always think about both computation and artistry.

- A brief description of the event
- The event details (where, when, and what to bring)
- A large, simple icon that describes or matches the type of event

Guidelines in mind, it's time to bring your UI to life. What features are you going to include? Which are you going to ignore?

REVIEW YOUR MOVES

• Were you thinking of the intended audience as you made UI design choices? How would you make your UI different to appeal to parents instead of kids?

• Art is never a competition—except when it is. Grab a friend and issue a challenge: Who can make the best UI? Both of you should pick a mock event and design a digital flyer for it, then show that flyer to someone else. Whose did they like more?

REDESIGN YOUR GUI

 *10–15 minutes*

 *1 player*

YOUR MISSION

You already know the cool background and slick icons that show up when you turn your computer on are part of your GUI. But what is the alternative? In older or more specialized operating systems, applications and software were opened using the command line interface (CLI). Instead of having nice icons that give users instant access, CLIs require users to have a deep knowledge of their machine and how it works. GUIs were a natural evolution from CLIs as consumers demanded easier ways to use their new technology—and the GUI has stuck around ever since. How could it be even further improved?

Your Gear
- **Drawing supplies**
- **Paper**

LET'S PLAY

Go ahead and turn on your computer. You've probably never thought about the details of your GUI, but give it a shot:
- What functions do you like?

- How does the menu look?
- Which icons do you like?

Redesign your GUI by drawing a better version of it. For example, you can redesign the icons for apps or software that you use regularly or put them in a different place for easy access.

REVIEW YOUR MOVES

- Show your changes to your friends and family. Would they use your new GUI, or do they prefer their normal look?
- Are your changes minor or major? Do you just want to change something's color, or do you want to change the way an entire layout functions?

CREATE A COLOR PALETTE

 10–15 minutes

 1 player

YOUR MISSION

Pretend you're an application developer: How do you keep people interested in your app? The first step is to make something that looks good. Using multiple colors is good, but you have to find a balance to appeal to more people. After all, would you want to use a website with a bunch of bright colors and different fonts all over the place? I doubt it!

Your Gear

- **Colored pencils, crayons, or markers**
- **Paper**

LET'S PLAY

Start off by placing some colored pencils, crayons, or markers onto a table. Then, pick three or four colors that you think go well together. Think about mixing and matching bright and neutral tones, but don't get crazy! Once you have your colors picked out, draw a small square on a piece of paper using each color. Think about how the colors look when you put them next to each other on a white surface. Do you want to change any? Once you have

The buttons, layout, functions, and overall feel in an application's UI are all critical components that can determine its success or failure. However, one of the first steps in the design process isn't to come up with any of these—it's to pick the overall color scheme. Why? Quite simply, as computer technology has continued to develop, users are very invested in being visually pleased with any piece of software they use. In the days of early computing, someone could get away with using plain black-and-white designs. Now, however, with infinite color combinations available, users want to have an experience that's both unique and vibrant.

your color template laid out, show it to your friends or parents! Ask for their feedback to see what you could do to make your app's color palette design even better.

REVIEW YOUR MOVES

• Now that you're a real designer, it's time to grab a friend and get serious. Each of you should pick a color palette and, using those colors, draw what your app's main screen might look like. Show your designs to another person—whose app would they like to use, just based on color?

• What kind of colors would you use for a fancy restaurant's take-out app? What about an app for your school? How about an app for your favorite video game?

GET TO KNOW YOUR USERS

 10–15 minutes

 2+ players

YOUR MISSION

One of the most important parts of the UX designer's job is to understand how the user feels about interacting with the technology in front of them. The people who download an app are going to be brand new to the software, while the designer has been working with it for months (or years). How on earth do they figure out what someone's reaction might be when they first download the app? Sometimes, the best way is to go directly to the user and conduct interviews!

Your Gear

- **Pencil**
- **Paper**

LET'S PLAY

To get started, you and your friend should write down answers to the following interview questions.

1. How long have you been using technology?
2. What was the first type of technology you can remember using? How old were you?
3. What do you think about smartphones?
4. Do you download any apps?
5. What apps do you use the most? Why?
6. Which internet browser do you use? Why do you like it?

7. What kind of technology do you use every day?

8. If you were on a desert island, what technology would you miss the most?

Once you're all done, compare your answers. How are your answers similar to each other? Now, using the same questions, interview someone else. Try to find someone of a different age, such as a parent, grandparent, or teacher. How do the adult's answers compare to yours and your friend's? Think about why they might have a different view of technology! More importantly, work together with your friends to think about how those different views of technology will influence the way they interact with a potential app.

REVIEW YOUR MOVES

• How do you think UX designers use this type of information to design apps and software?

• Ready to apply your new knowledge? Using the answers you and your friend gathered from someone else, each of you should design a UX that would appeal to that person. See whose UX that person prefers!

SPEC IT OUT!

 10–15 minutes

 1 player

YOUR MISSION

If you could create the ultimate piece of software to help you be more successful at school, what would it do? The first step to making a killer app is to think about its specifications, or specs. After all, you can't design your UI if you don't know what your app does!

- What is a situation in which the app would be used and what problem would it solve?
- What are the inputs? The actions? The outputs?

Your Gear

- **Pencil**
- **Paper**

LET'S PLAY

Start dreaming up some awesome specs for your ultimate student app. Keep these four key aspects of designing software in mind:

1. Use scenario: When and where will the app be used? What problem is it intended to solve?

2. Inputs: What data will the user provide for the app to work with?

3. Actions: What actions will the app take based on the inputs? What work does the app do? What steps are necessary to prepare the appropriate output?

4. Outputs: What data will the app provide back to the user after doing its work?

Thinking of ways to design an application is a great way to break into the world of computer science. Every programmer has to start somewhere, and it can be very helpful to look at a project—with no coding involved—and come up with a software solution. Considering use scenarios, inputs, actions, and outputs is a real step in the programming process, and this activity is your first step down the path of computational thinking, or learning to think like a computer.

These are not the only important considerations for your app, but they will help define the way you create a UI and UX to fit. Once you've got all that figured out, write a user story for the program. The user story should describe the typical user and their problem, identify

how the app will solve the problem for them, and then describe how they'd use it. The point of writing this user story is to give you a better idea of the kind of UX you should design!

REVIEW YOUR MOVES

• You can't think about yourself all the time! Your software design should keep in mind that other people are going to be looking at—and using—your hard work, so it needs to make just as much sense to them as it does to you.

• Writing out how an app will work is great, but that's not enough to make it real. Think about other information you'd need to really bring your awesome app to life!

THERE'S AN APP FOR THAT! PART 1

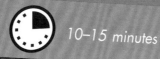 10–15 minutes

 1 player

YOUR MISSION

There are way too many apps available for computers, tablets, and smartphones. If you can imagine it, there's probably an app for that! Designing an app, however, is serious business—even before it gets coded. You'll have to come up with a new way of doing things if you want to be successful.

Your Gear

- **Drawing supplies**
- **Paper**

LET'S PLAY

Think of a problem in the world. Maybe it's a problem that you deal with every day, like having to do chores. Or maybe it's bigger, like world hunger. Or maybe it's somewhere in between—it's up to you!

Problem in mind, come up with an idea for an app that can make it a little easier to deal with. Describe how the app works, how people would use it, and what it would look like. Then, draw how you'd like your app's UI to look. It better look good if you want it to stand out on the app store!

REVIEW YOUR MOVES

• Share your app designs with a few friends or your parents and ask for their feedback. Would they use it? How would they change it?

• Can your friends come up with a better way of solving your problem? Ask them to do this activity, too, and see what kind of app they come up with. Did they make any improvements to your original UI design?

THERE'S AN APP FOR THAT! PART 2

 10–15 minutes

 1 playe

YOUR MISSION

Now that you have an idea of how you'd like your new app to look, it's time to explore how you might try to make it a reality!

Your Gear

- **Pencil**
- **Paper**

LET'S PLAY

Start off by copying the There's an App for That! Organizer from page 25 onto a separate sheet of paper. With your idea from There's an App for That! Part 1, use the organizer to walk yourself through four rules for coding:

Rule 1: Coders must know what they want the computer to do and write a plan.

Rule 2: Coders must use special words to tell the computer to accept input, make choices, and take action.

Rule 3: Coders need to think about what tasks can be put into a group.

Rule 4: Coders must explore the environment and understand how it works.

By now, you've probably recognized some common elements between an app's function and its UX. As you fill out the organizer and think about these rules, make sure to take notes on how your UI and UX will fit into the overall design process. You don't know how to code just yet, but keep this organizer in mind—maybe someday, your killer app will become a reality.

REVIEW YOUR MOVES

- Think about putting your new software on the app store. What would you do if it got really great reviews? Or, what if some people really didn't like it? Making people happy is a key component of UX design.

- If you're a coder, you better get used to working on really long-term projects. How would you improve your app over time to keep people interested? Think about ways to refresh your UI (for example, what about including pumpkins during the fall?).

THERE'S AN APP FOR THAT! ORGANIZER

Describe your idea for an app. What will it do? Whom will it help?	
What special UX features will you need to include? How will this impact the UI?	
What tasks can be grouped together? Why?	
Can you imagine any possible problems with your app? What could go wrong?	

WORLD BUILDING

 10–15 minutes

 *2+ players*

YOUR MISSION

Some of your favorite video games are probably made using procedural generation. This type of program can create infinite worlds that follow a certain set of rules. *Minecraft* is a good example of this type of game— it tries to place different types of terrain (such as forests and deserts) either close together or far away. To help make bordering regions look different, game maps use different colors. This is a good lesson in general design. Organizing a game map is sort of like designing software overall: Some things should be placed next to some things, but far away from others.

Your Gear

- **Pencil**
- **Colored pencils, crayons, or markers**
- **Paper**

LET'S PLAY

To get started, every player needs to draw their own unique maps—without coloring them in—based on the examples from page 28. Trade maps with the other player and get ready to race. The goal is to color in the map as fast as possible, but there are a few rules:

1. Any area that shares a border can't have the same coloring as its neighbor.
2. You have to use as few colors as possible.

To win, you not only need to color the quickest, you also have to make sure you're following these rules. For example, if the fastest player had two neighboring sections both colored red, the other player will win!

If you're struggling with ways to prevent colors from touching, the best way to get started is to look at all of the intersections. On your map, how many regions intersect at any one point? When regions intersect, that meeting point determines the minimum number of colors necessary for the map. You need at least as many colors as there are sections at that area—and probably more. Find an intersection to start with and grow out from there, trying different color combinations! Eventually, you'll be able to figure out a combination that works for your particular map.

REVIEW YOUR MOVES

• How long did it take you to figure out the right number of colors to use? A game like *Minecraft* has to make thousands of similar decisions instantaneously!

• You probably stopped to think: "Why can't neighboring areas share a color?" They need to have different colors so that someone doesn't get confused about the type of area they're in. Part of UX design is making things easy to understand, so separating regions by color is a great solution.

GUESS WHO?

YOUR MISSION

UX and UI designers have to design the look of an app or website to meet the needs of the person using it. They have to think of how the user is going to interact with all of the functions. After all, if someone doesn't like a website, chances are high they'll never return—and that's not good! One of the most important features of a piece of software is the user experience; people will always be drawn toward a product that is the easiest to look at and use.

LET'S PLAY

To start off, give each player four index cards—these will be their user cards. Each player should draw a different hypothetical app design on one side of each of their index cards. These apps can be anything, such as a game, a homework help app, a game show app, etc. Each app design should show what the main screen of an app would look like.

On the back of each of these user cards, each player should describe a hypothetical person who might use the app. For example: "Lindsey uses this app to shop for clothes." Also on the back, each player should write a short description of what their app does. Don't show the other player the back of these cards!

Once each player has created their user cards, the game can begin. Here's how it works:

1. Player A will select one of their user cards:
   - Player A will need to hold the card so they can see the description of the app, while Player B can only see the design.
   - Player A should not read their description aloud or give any clues as to who their user is.
2. Player B will analyze the app design. Only asking yes or no questions, Player B will begin to guess who the user is and what they might use the app for. Player B should base their questions on the design of the UI. But there's a catch—each player will only have twenty questions for the entire game!

3. Once Player B correctly guesses the user, it is Player B's turn to present a user card. Player A will then try to guess the new user! Repeat the game until one player runs out of questions or all the cards have been drawn. The player with the most correct guesses wins! If there's a tie, the person with more questions left is the winner.

REVIEW YOUR MOVES

• Were there any designs that could have been made for multiple users? What about the design made it appealing to different kinds of people?
• Ideally, this game would always end in a tie. Why? Because good UI design means an app should be easily identified immediately. If your opponent can't figure out what your app is for, that's a problem!

VIDEO, TEXTING, AND CHATTING, OH MY!

 *10–15 minutes*

 *2 players*

YOUR MISSION

What are all the ways people can communicate? In person, writing notes, emailing, online chat, video chat, through video games, on the phone, texting, taking pictures, and more! If you're going to be a UX designer, you need to have excellent communication skills to gather the information needed to design new apps and software. UX designers are responsible for gathering data from their potential users—and how would they do that without communicating?

LET'S PLAY

Your Gear

- **Drawing supplies**
- **Paper**

To start off, grab a friend and sit back to back. Make sure you both have a piece of paper and a pencil. Decide who's going first—that person will begin drawing a picture of anything they want. At the same time, that person will tell the other player how to draw the same picture. Neither person can turn around or look at what the other person is drawing. The

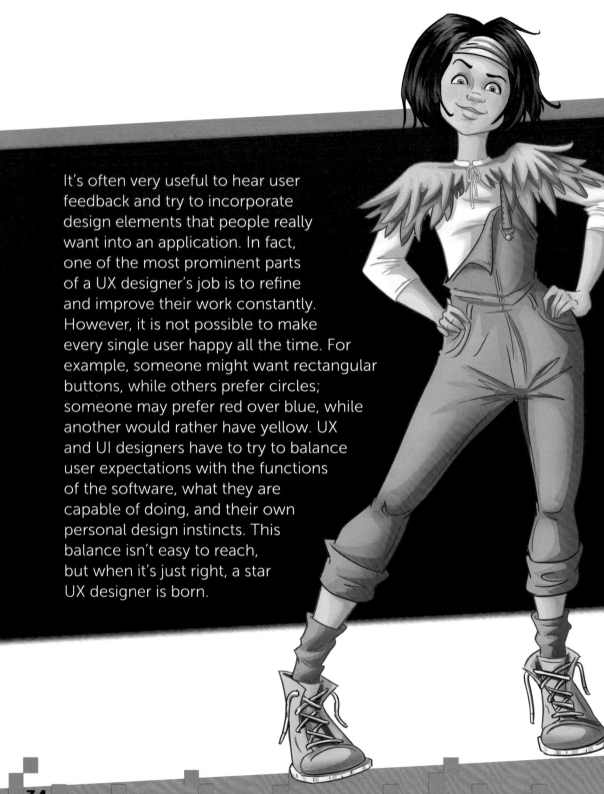

It's often very useful to hear user feedback and try to incorporate design elements that people really want into an application. In fact, one of the most prominent parts of a UX designer's job is to refine and improve their work constantly. However, it is not possible to make every single user happy all the time. For example, someone might want rectangular buttons, while others prefer circles; someone may prefer red over blue, while another would rather have yellow. UX and UI designers have to try to balance user expectations with the functions of the software, what they are capable of doing, and their own personal design instincts. This balance isn't easy to reach, but when it's just right, a star UX designer is born.

drawer can only use their words to give instructions! After the drawer has finished drawing and explaining how to draw, compare the two drawings. How do they look?

Finally, switch roles and have the other player give the drawing instructions this time. I bet it was easier the second time! This activity is similar to the kind of guesswork that goes into the UX design process. Software developers often have an idea of what they want their app to look like, and they have to balance that against the instructions given by their potential audience, their supervisors' expectations, and more. Creating a good UX isn't easy, and the best designers make sure to take their audience's preferences into account!

REVIEW YOUR MOVES

• Why is it important to make sure others can understand what you want designed?

• After you compared your drawing with your friend's, did you notice anything they did totally wrong? Whose fault was that—did you give bad instructions, or did they misinterpret you?

BECOME THE UX DESIGNER!

 15–20 minutes

 *2 players*

YOUR MISSION

If you were making an application, you'd want people to download and use it. But who's going to use an app that doesn't run well or look good? To make sure people have a good time using software, UX designers have to understand their users. But creating a combination of accessibility and performance can be a complex process!

Your Gear

- **Pencil**
- **Paper**

LET'S PLAY

To start off, you and a friend should each make up a potential user for a new piece of software. Think about the following questions as you create the user:

- What do they like? This could be anything, from favorite colors to favorite sports teams.
- What is their job? You should also think about why they work in this job.

36

- What are some of their favorite things? This should be more than one thing—everyone has a lot of interests!
- What do they want to accomplish? This is closely related to their job and what their UX should help them do.

Once you're all done with that, trade users with your friend. After you've traded, explain some of the background behind your user. Now that you each have a user to make software for, you'll become UX designers. Based on the user information you've got, design an experience just for that user! Think about these steps as you design:

1. Preplanning: You completed this step by asking questions about your partner's user! This gives you a solid start.
2. Exploration: What does the user want to use their app to do? Be sure to think about things that are important for them to accomplish their goal or job!

3. Design: What does your user's perfect UX look like? Stop and check the information you have about your user to make sure the new design will work for them!

4. Quality: How will your user take advantage of the new software you're designing? Answer this question and you'll be able to find any holes in your logic or plans. Take time to go back and fix any errors or missing items!

5. Feedback: Show your UX package to your friend. What do they think of it? During this step of the process, it is important for you to have an open mind and be open to the constructive criticism your friend presents. Remember, your job as a UX designer is to make the user happy!

REVIEW YOUR MOVES

• If you did any steps out of order, how would your UX be different? Do you wish you had done things differently?

• No single UX will be perfect for every single person—after all, there are billions of people in the world! How can your design work for a large group of people with different tastes?

GIVE ME A HAND

 10–15 minutes

 1 player

YOUR MISSION

One way to help you think about general design details is to step back from software and look, instead, at hardware. Many aspects of UX and UI design (such as location of buttons, functions, and overall feel) can also be applied to the field of robotics. If you had a chance to invent an automaton (a robot that can do work), what task would you want it to complete for you? Given that task, what type of hand attachment would the automaton need?

Your Gear

- **Pencil**
- **Drawing supplies**
- **Paper**

LET'S PLAY

Get started by identifying the problem you want your automaton to solve. For example, it could be a household chore such as vacuuming, doing the dishes, or taking out the garbage. Write a description of the problem and the specific task to be completed by the automaton. This is similar to describing a problem for an app to solve.

Now that you've identified your task, what's the best tool for completing it? Imagine that your automaton has a customized hand attachment that is specifically designed to complete the task involved—and the person doing the specific designing is you.

- What are the requirements of the task in terms of specific directions of work?
- Will it involve grasping? Moving? Other types of work actions?
- Go back to your written description of the task and explore it in much greater detail. What are the exact actions to be taken?

Now you're ready to invent! Treat the detailed description of the task as the specs for your

The study of robotics is where the fields of engineering and computer science meet. Creating a robot that can do anything—let alone a complex task—is a remarkable achievement, and it can only be reached by combining a deep knowledge of programming, design, and engineering skills. As robot usage continues to increase across various industries, the marriage of software and hardware is more important than ever. There are dozens of apps tied to consumer-grade robots, and each has a different UI and UX, and many are meant to accomplish different things. The common thread between them all, however, is an attention to the small details required to make a machine move.

automaton's hand. Try to draw a hand that would best complete the task for the problem you want to solve. What kind of functions and features does your hand have? Write these down next to your drawing, and try to identify what specific parts of your new hand are contributing to those functions and features. When you're done, you'll probably be looking at something that resembles the GUI for a smartphone app to control a robot!

REVIEW YOUR MOVES

• Would you want your new automaton to help you with other things? Will it be able to if you made your hand attachment too specific? On the other hand, will your automaton be able to complete its main task if it isn't specific enough?

• Show your design to a friend and see if they can help you improve it. Maybe they know a few shortcuts it could take to make the task even easier! This is another parallel between UX and UI design and robotics—it's always important to gather user feedback.

GLOSSARY

accessibility The degree to which a piece of software is easy to use for a beginner.

application A kind of software designed to complete specific tasks.

color palette A selection of colors chosen to complement each other.

command line interface A user interface that allows users to use text commands for running programs.

desktop The computer screen that contains various graphical user interface items.

developer A coder who conceives of or creates software, applications, etc.

features The tools presented by a piece of software.

functions The things that an application, button, etc., are capable of doing.

graphical Describing something that is represented by an image.

input The data given to an application by a user.

neutral Describing a color that is neither too bright nor too dull.

operating system The overarching set of styles, functions, etc., of a computer.

output The data given to a user by an application.

procedural generation A type of game-making that randomly creates maps, etc., based on a set of rules or procedures.

shortcut A button or icon that can be clicked to launch an application.

specifications The detailed list of a software's functions and features.

user experience The way a user feels about and interacts with a computer program; includes user interface design, accessibility, etc.

user interface The set of systems and functions within which a computer user accomplishes their tasks.

vibrant Describing a color that is powerful and attractive.

FURTHER READING

BOOKS

Hinton, Kerry. *Becoming a User Interface and User Experience Engineer.* New York, NY: Rosen Publishing, 2018.

Lyons, Heather, and Dan Crisp. *Develop Helpful Apps.* London, UK: Wayland, 2017.

Winquist, Gloria, and Matt McCarthy. *Coding iPhone Apps for Kids: A Playful Introduction to Swift.* San Francisco, CA: No Starch Press, 2017.

Young Rewired State. *Get Coding!: Learn HTML, CSS, and JavaScript and Build a Website, App, and Game.* Illustrated by Duncan Beedie. Somerville, MA: Candlewick Press, 2017.

WEBSITES

Hopscotch

https://www.gethopscotch.com

Provides a platform for block-based coding, including software, tutorials, and examples from users.

Interaction Design Foundation

https://www.interaction-design.org/literature/topics/ui-design

Provides a definition of user interface design, including multimedia examples and tips for the design process.

INDEX